definitions uprising

definitions uprising

melissa christine goodrum

The New York Quarterly Foundation, Inc.
New York, New York

NYQ Books™ is an imprint of The New York Quarterly Foundation, Inc.

The New York Quarterly Foundation, Inc.
P. O. Box 2015
Old Chelsea Station
New York, NY 10113

www.nyqbooks.org

Copyright © 2013 by melissa christine goodrum

All rights reserved. No part of this book may be used or reproduced in any manner whatsoever without written permission of the author. This book is a work of fiction.

First Edition

Set in Cochin
Layout and Design by melissa christine goodrum
Cover Design by Raymond P. Hammond
Cover Image by Gabriel Padilha | www.gabrielpadilha.com

Library of Congress Control Number: 2013952378

ISBN: 978-1-935520-78-8

definitions uprising

Acknowledgments

Thanks to D.D. Conway for playing the great bear, W. Whitman, growling on an LP; Mr. Leith & Mrs. Hamilton for introducing many of the classics; Bob Holman for introducing my living elders; Ammiel Alcalay for opening the door to Dorn and the outriders; Lou Asekoff for handing me Yeats' "Vision," Chip Livingston for pushing ever so gently; Cornell University for existing as a Tarzanian nuero-breeding ground; Lauren Wheeler and Patrick Sylvain for warm inspiration and loving encouragement; my poet Gurus: P. Smith, A. Waldman, B. Coultas, L. Jarnot, and to Sapphire, who always keeps her promises (without these honest, sparkling, political and feminine voices, I never would have moved to and remained in nyc); Mike Whalen for reading with care and to my ed go for his creativity, patience, humor & love.

Thanks to all my Humanities teachers, professors, poet friends, art-making peers and beloved family. *If it takes a village to raise a child, it took all of you to help this poet fly.*

And to the editors of the following journals, where poems included in this manuscript were first published:

The New York Quarterly, v.65, 2009, "Object"

canwehaveourballback?, July 2005, "sound" and "the exhibitor of words"

*for Christine P. Goodrum
& Aunty Rose*

contents

la invita   1

i

signore hopkins, the old eye-sore   4
eye lines   5
eyes   7

ii

to think sleeping   10
dream sonnet   11
dream lines   13
dream proem   17

iii

the exhibitor of words   21
lip lines   22
lips   25

iv

sound   29
screaming lines   30
screams   32

v

victims   35
finger lines   36
fingers   37

vi

stripped & bleeding	41
skin lines	42
skin	43

vii

wish & want	49

viii

in the galleys	53
god lines	54
god, the prophet	55

ix

little explosions	59
stars in lines	60

x

solpugid, as applied to the marigold	65
sun lines	66
sun	67

xi

object	71
moon lines	72
defining moon	73

xii

baby blue	77
mam's blues	78
deafening blue	79

"Are you trying to 'describe' me, boy?"

—Edward Dorn, *Gunslinger*

from the back of a Pinto, in a yellow-bellied desert...
---

la invita

Oh, screw them. Oh, knobby-kneed rapists.
Oh, kneaded bread. Oh, AIDS. Oh, Holly
wood. Oh, homeless boxes. Oh, something
terrible. Oh, children. Oh, sigh. Oh, the sifted
edges. Oh, understanding. Oh, holy standard.
Oh, sacred & sexy cow. Oh, 40 acres.
  Oh, mustang. Oh, national plagues.
   Oh, avian flu. Oh, little blue wingers.
    Oh, electric globalization. Oh, stale
     stereotype. Oh, English. Oh, up round
     sun. Oh, out definition.
        Oh, so tender.   Oh, blue warbler.
         Oh, ink & publicize. Oh, yard-tags.
          Oh, wealth. Oh, ye gods. Oh, open
           flesh. Oh, artists balking. Oh, finite
            & astral ink. Oh, victims. Oh, holy days.

Oh! Eye-Siren. Oh, indigenous moon.
    Oh, be a woman. Oh, be a man.
      Oh, war. Oh, home. Oh, desert sons.
        Oh, ye worshipers. Oh, I ego.

    Oh, me crime. Oh, without you religious interest.
      Oh, god-ness. Oh, god wars. Oh, Jimmy
        God-slot. Oh, play it loudly.
          Oh, public stages.
          Oh, exhibitor of words.
    Oh, witnesses. Oh, jazz cats.

Oh, virgins, make much of planes.
Oh, puritanical laws. Oh, impelling protest.

Oh, action. Oh, remember auction. Oh, the drums will wail.
Oh, affluent fat cheats. Oh, Katrina. Oh, Sandy.
Oh, water. Oh, fire.
Oh, wind. Oh, death.

Oh, honest indicator. Oh, listener.
Oh, reader. Oh, peas roll.
Oh, enter here.

i   **eyes**
___

signore hopkins, the old eyesore

warm lichen, listen,
listen & she
will make you weep.
do not dare
go into sleep.
see the eye-star, noir.
check on the veiled roping structure,
the sweeping hull's glare,
the hermit's herring of a holler—
like ocellus, little insect wings.

you have an eye for twilight
& it will find you.

Storm, the lightning
flashes & you remember
to cure. You open the door,
stand in the wind
a well-defined eye,
open your own
& let the eyes flush, flash!

The lightening comes —
the center
of this drum. Metal melding
your soggy shoes,
lightening looks
into *your* eyes
& she looks
severely, *My damnéd eyes*.

She sees the dry eye
your river (home)
beginning to hummingbird
& run. She sees
the ingénue in you.
The peacock's tail
shines eyes iridescent,
like ocellus or little
insect wings. She sees,
she knows.
She discerns the sea,
the ship in your eye.

She knows this land,
the green budding within
your womb. An eye
of yellow on your skin
does not yet bear
your un-witty name.

You have an eye
for twilight
& it will find you.

She is mechanical
or a electrical device
resembling voice,
a quasi-personified object.

& you will rue
the day you found your fancy
for more autonomy, freedom
within the eye, on the inside,
near the outside,
in leopard print
& a porno-whale plastered
sickly with high & royal blue.

You, you will know
the beautifully checkered war cry.
Oh! Eye-Siren. She
keeps an eye
on you. She has an eye
for you & with a gleam
or the sinking in a twinkle.

Blood blind, glad
& loving, you will meet
her, eye to eye.

G.M. Hopkins, the old eye-sore, proclaimed that we should not bake unlawful, or 'mere eye-rhymes', what right does he have to say that if it rhymes in my eye, it is not a sound? With even one glass eye I could see that rhyme. It had a round shape, a brown center with white lines & the delicate black clack of an exoskeleton.

What about the eye-Syren? Warm lichen, listen. She is pleasing to the ear & not harmful in the eye—does that make her any less striking? No. Listen & she will make you weep. Do not dare go into sleep. In, she just will not. Just do not. D'ot count those plastic sheep. Do no. Do no harm. I do no harm. Look at me. See me bite. See the eye-star, noir. It is a blinkin' spry near my body's thigh. Stop.

In the golden heaviest of centers there is an extra black pupil & he is learning how to lie. He is tired of tie winking & wants his shy liner back. Why only one lid & two pupils. He is the jealous sort. These eyes donut always lie, on their heads. Check on the veiled roping structure, the sweeping hull's glare, the hermit's herring of a holler: malicious, alone & eye-gouging. The other law-mother is transfixed & seeking an attractive rhythm, one that will permanently remove the other pupil.

She will publicize. It will be the sight of advertisements this year. On everyone's shop-right list, I am sure of the hook. Even you will sew one, if your granddaughter wants one, you will remove the dusty basket from the attic & open up that sewing kit you bought because it was on sale. Up & down, use an eye & hook to finish the job. Stop.

Now you will sob, because you are afraid of the dwarf-holes deep-set in glassy buttons. Because you have not eaten & the bread is hard, moldy, & the eyes in the bread bleed, having been freshly beaten, nice & plump. Holes, whores, soft women, kneaded bread, the eye of a needle, the blinker in the eye of the storm. Use your indicator. The oven is ticking. Time! There is no blooming bastard in the sphere of your warm oven. Nine, & you will weep some more, for the seat of electrocuting intelligence & the crafted light of a skulking private eye.

ii   dreams

to think sleeping

they carried their aching
west & rode sallow mules

their eyes marvelously open:
while a meatless monkey,
with palmed mechanical hands
was clapping, there is eye-lime dust
& a tree. you want
to climb
them, a national plague of pocket-pickers
& red-leather wallet lickers,
a curly brown afro & two-toned shoes.

these feathers are frightening in color.
odor is thick carbon, then colorless
but the taste is grey—
awfully muted, sweat-putrid & grey.

dream sonnet

    In the eye pond
        try tasting twice   *dream*
       the same name,
          fly cards, diamonds   *fly fast*
come on self-spitting & lurid,
    a scream's atonal   *some scam*
        a sharp wheel burn, a pitch,
      the lonely name.   *flamboyant*
     One with heads,
two without beds.   *& unreal*

     Alice, the little one   *girl*
       the card-men saved.
   You chase your last   *dream*
fiend, in uniform speed,
  You will stand,   *stacked*
    in this black-sacked city,
       so neat or well-behaved.   *pills*
         but blond & still growing,
  as some overgrown weed.   *pluck*

    Though wide & wet   *circles*
the cross-drums wail.

There is simply greatness,   *around porcelain*
   a gold door & kiss tree.
 Alice may look now   *purloin*
    & loathe & love.

   Again, she may guzzle   *a choice*
make herself be~wild.
No blue (downhill) pill,   *to carry*
    or strawberry (up) pill
to sort out, floss or shelve.   *be awake*

But she may sharply
    inhale, and harvest   *hard as hail*
   dew ponds, or lip 'n
linger near sable moon-cherries.   *her tale*

Think   sleeping vigor,
depth, wry &   silken fragile,

(too dry paper   rattles)
&   changes levels, places
for the plane-field, geometry.

Places you   don't know
anyone's name
& don't   remember when

you   came. Sounds too slow
in the dream…sped up
with the pitch of   scream

colors   charge
too bright, they   come
fast like lone wheels in a brigade,

so cave man   made,
rough & locked,
(but, useless without ego)

so in scores the peoples   came
to   dream things with their heads

without heads, under bed
& in closet they   carried
their 40 acres

the claws, the claw
there & the eyes
        hold, body parts   bleed white
ashy arms that   may crawl
on their own

snot-hosed kids

        wipe   &   foretell,
(this   a call to the vein: wake up)
        wake up without difficulty,

the dream　　　would never
　　　be a dream

in books you　　　can dream
with your eyes　sewn
marvelously open & a plot

there, it　　　is turning,
page under page…under…

Clouds　　　will chase your dream
with uniform speed.

The unreal　　whip　　crack
that meatless monkey
　　　is screaming out.

Ode to his rancid head
& mechanical hands
　　　still clapping

Oh, these native dreams,
post-coital languages,
furried tongues　　　imbued

with　　licking,　　　lapping up
emissions, air & the flotsam
green sky

a monkey's lip　　　is screaming
&　　speaking a lewd language

I　　haven't learned
there　　　is no dictionary,

no madness　　to amplify,
　　　this sounding, an endless byte.

Left, mind　　swinging
&　　counting to ten,
eep…eep.

❋❋❋

A robot necromancer
       walking Nevada

where they   assign silver
marriage licenses easy

now,   see Sri Lanka
so your monkey   waves
from his postcard.

       Sing,   Sing
       sound around
your hollow mouth

no, you   may not speak.
just   wave
& the plastic   will hamper
this exchange.

This   is a sight
the night dream,   dig on.

& Oh, the drums   will wail,
      pounding loud & delicious,

when whetted fancy   runs
freely, deliberately, you   will stand

to   see the pregnancy
(below your toes)
in a narrow yellow valley,

there   is greatness, dust
& a tree.

You   want to climb
tree. This urge
     is strong. Your thirst
     is a national plague. This reverie,
these bonked unrealities,

a gradation of fools,
as marionettes   ticking
heads back 'n forth,   clicking
on the light,   clapping
to the beat

of joe smith,   turning
their votes into jokes,
their   wriggling throats

        strung into English
        speaking "Globulization"
& gobble, gobble.

This   is no Gertrude Stein.
This   is not noun-sense,

or the impersonal construction.

Now please just   sit down
&   do the acrobatics,
i.e., avant-garde arithmetic.

Dream-consciousness + Content will become X dream-habit when you divide dream-imagery into the many three o'clocks.

Answer: You've been salted & dream-ridden.

In this dream-city of pocket-pickers & red-leather wallet lickers, they are heavy-footed when they ferret home, re-forming & snatching at these complex visuals.

In wide & webbed circles sea come hallucinatory beads & cerulean pea-plucked feathers. They arrive at the velour curtains of the so-called dream teller.

They ask for a steel-drum dream-cross. That sundown place X said was 'between birth & dying'. She will look up & foretell of pain & love & joy & mirth.

Echoing, until you're back. You, be contiguously dream-fed by your only son. He becomes a hover dreamboat & a curly brown afro

& one two-toned shoe. Hang lids drowsily. He will never listen with no headphones on, alone, in tilting radiance. Stereotypes become frightening within his spectrum. Odor is devised, & re-invented thus, in filmy black & white.

Smell kiss: this forgotten noir.

iii   lips
---

the exhibitor of words

undervalued & strapped
to a chair,
like a bulged blossom
& two wounds lipping.
this four-eyed spell-maker,
like musical lids opening
the window
of a closed shop
inside a cave,
he plays the pipes.
he is a volcano

where a hooded wizard
plucks a chicken
& feeds
its lips to the mage.

    Open flesh
    structures. Yes, she have four
    this seems vulgar some   how?

                  It is not just some lip
    I am trying to give you
    yet,   it,   this, the lower lip,
    it brings sweet

sweet remember:
    Red lips Pink lips
    Biting lips Tasting lips
    Licking lips   Fucking lips

                inside of thigh
                wet Women lips
    returning
                to the soft other cavities

    of mouth.   The exhibitor
    of words   flapping lips,
                        like lids
    of a window
    of a shop   inside a cave

    where a wizard plucks a chicken
                & feeds its lips
                to the mage.

    The hooded magus
    undervalued in Latin & strapped
    to the chair.

    He play the pipes

        well,
        without his upper lip
        cleft

    this all would sound numb
            in hell.
                    I am on the lip

                of something

                                        on the edge of gravel
                                of under-sanding

        a present.   This false button   s lip

        read a lip
                                A punishment

        to the lovely lip.
        Those without lips   envy
        those with lips.
                        They   pay
        fat money to be left
        stuck   smiling plastic

        A sentence found unworthy
of heart

        Those white lights
        in Hollywood set
        the holy standard.

        Things, young females   flip
        through, they try to   uncover
        the right   shade,

                        to understand
                        the taste
                                of someone else
                                's ssspit.

        As his young lips   near

        hers...She tilts
        her head   back
                                waits for magic

        a four-eyed mage
        will make her
                                left leg leap,
        she knows.
        He leans

                                        back, just before
                        making contact
            lip-sync-she
                                        bites
                                        pink whale lard
            off of her lip
                                        tries to hide
            a smirk
            looks down
            the round lip
                                        to her Mary Janes.

            He curls
            his thin lip round
            sheer steel
            braces   a damsel tied
                                to the railroad track.

            He was expecting

            a pout, like   the bulged blossom plant.

            Lip-position   good,
                                four lips
            smile,   breathe
            in.

She will not give
                                satisfaction. She knows
                                the rule,
                                he, a volcano.
            His eyes hang
                                onto her
                                painted lips.
            A moment,
                                pause.
            She licks one.
            He looks.   She looks.
            They kiss   now. Two wounds
                                lipping.

Flesh structures, yes, I have four. Labium, labellum, the reference seems vehicular somehow. It is not just any slip. & yet, it, this, the lower lip, it brings rapture & a buckling blue moonlit memory. Inside of the high, wet spooning hips, a famous poet once said 'her honey sweet lips' to this, the currant topic of bottled conversation:

> The exhibitor of words, with flapping and bulbous lips is to be eaten, drunk or spoken. Where a punishment of the lovely lip is a 14-gauge silver ring passed through the present lip of shiny & swimming bait. Those without glossy & decorated flapping lips envy those with location. Pretences I find unworthy of re-hearing. Lady-like lessons echo, around white & stolen statues surrounding the patented Vatican City. Thinly robed males flip through barefoot, try to uncover the right shade of haughty, to understand the test of someone else's hermetic fits.

As this young rhythm nears a monk's mental lip, he tilts his head back & waits for the magic. Perhaps the angel in the snow-globe will awaken to write a four-paged symphony. Yes, a glowing muse will make his left-brain leap. He leans back, just before making contact, lip-sync. He tries to hide his smirk, and then looks down, at the rhetorical discovery of his songbook. He curls his thin lip around clear & historical grails, expecting a lip-crackle or life spouts, in staccato, like the bulged blossom plant. Instead, he finds the writer.

She will not give him an unsung satisfaction. A clacking-sound she makes with her pen tip, she knows the rules. The imprint is made. He is not the savior. His eyes hang onto her painted lips. She licks one. He. She. They are relating at the lips. Oh, fluid, organs of speech, lip-quiver, lip-link, lip-lock.

iv   screams
___

sound

a great grey elephant,
a heavy brown sound
a fjord of dirty monkeys
loud (like something being killed)

the red mahogany fiddle
is a thought, it screams
in the middle

like your stomach after
a bit of raw meat,
rapists & red fiddles,
just take the bread & go.

a small sound resounds
beneath window, a pond,
imagine this piercing   & hallow:

        a woman seeing the pursuer

  (what if he were handsome?
  her uncle? What then?)

Brown box-men almost never ask.
Or say, 'just take the bread & go'.
Can't warm brown bread incur a scream? a scream of pleasure, a little
bittle of a scream,
     high-pitched   & not unpleasant.
                                   the place you crave to be? Where
                                   do these beasts be?
Great grayish elephants,
 & dirty furry monkeys
                              Ne'er in NYC
           we do not shriek with joy,
           when children think
           they are the center in
           a zebra's painted universe
they scream   they,   within   soldiered
entrapments
standing on a pawnshop's Elizabethan golden lace
in terror. with terror.

Not with pleasure.
 & that is worth defining.

Someone might put you in a cage
on top of the refrigerator. Forget to feed you
for days.
You would never sound
like the fiddle. Think,
you would sound

like being killed.
[Over & over & over again]

The red mahogany fiddle screams

    & no one seems to mind   that   it   screams   high
                     & it screams in the middle.

               Like your stomach
               after a bit of raw meat &
               something else, unsavory, but valued.

It screams. Your lover
turns around, holds you
 & laughs.   What is amusing about a scream?

What is this outside alley doing to woman?
Street-walker?
Meddler?
Noisemaker?
Oh, the bad & un-glorified hymen taker,
a raw theft dries in unkempt aversions to night,
& the dirtied ground rolls.
a scream, a second
a courageous fighter plane, peaks

at car wheels burning out   tar
a scream of headache
               tearing through blue veins.
               Sit here & imagine,
                       reverie
                   about monkeys, creeping don
            juans & red fiddles
Something terrible is happening,
something toxic inside of lemon-shaped garbage bins.
A rat, a mouse, a mask
 & an animal scavenging
his nose in the dirty bins,
                     all the bits & pieces.

    Tearing off the lid
    scratching never uncut claws
    against the silver mental can.
    He be the carrion thief,
    a nippy purse-snatcher.

A small sound resounds & I stir in my bed. Just beneath the windowpane, I imagine this piercing hollow: a woman sees her pursuer. But what if he were handsome? Her uncle? What then? Why can't warm brown bread incur a gullet-y scream, a scream of pleasure, a little bittle of a scream, high-pitched, but not unpleasant. Just the place you crave to be. Where do the beasts want to be? (Great grey-ish elephants, heavy brown & dirty furry monkeys?) Certainly not here. Never in New York City. They do not shriek with joy. When children think they are the center of a zebra's universe, they scream from within thorned entrapments. No matter how nice you may think that quaint birdcage, no matter how expensive you purchased the damn thing for…They scream at the golden lace in terror. Not with pleasure & that is worth defining. How would you feel in a cage on top of the refrigerator? Not fed for days? I do not think you would sound like a fiddle. I think you would sound like something being killed. Over & over & over again.

The red mahogany fiddle is a nicer thought. It screams & no one seems to mind. It screams high & it screams in the middle. Like your stomach after a bit of raw meat & something else unsavory, but valued. It screams & your lover turns around, holds you & laughs. Your lover is amused. What is amusing about a scream? & what is this woman doing outside of my bedroom? Street-walker? What does she want with me & my thoughts? Meddler, noisemaker, yes that is actually the first thought: pillaging & theft into the night, on the dirty ground, for only a scream of a second. If I were to lean out, like a courageous fighter plane & take a scream, a peak.

But would I call the police if I saw something like that? The scream, car wheels turning out tar-scum. He would get away & I would have to scream of a headache tearing through my veins, like the carrion's writhing flesh. What if this attacker is giving his victim a disease? Why do I sit here & think, imagine, dream about monkeys, hunters & red fiddles while something terrible is happening? Something terrible is inside of the garbage bins—insert a rat, a mouse, & a clown mask. An animal is scavenging his nose into my dusty bins, yes, all the bits & pieces. Tearing off the lid…scratching his uncut nails against the silver metal can & seeking last night's burnt toaster bits. He is a thief. Just like the purse-snatcher. That settles it. I am screaming. I am screaming. Call the birds for I, the poet, at last, am up to no good.

v   fingers

victims

the smallest members
of an opulent body
of stuttering white starfish
or flying finger-fish,
a faulted flinger in the pie,

finger-snapping, spinning, speaking,
little silver-smiths bringing life

those little wingers

oh, blot, blot onto the long & slender plot
see! the hand.
it never miscounts sea faces
with pasty & powdered blues.

Tiny terminal
member hands
the itching tribe
paper-cut
scribe
ever-healing
wigglers, they
page dance
wing touch
feisty feeler
one-oh-one
forefinger
why not after?
index, number one,
listing or listening?
middle-finger,
new outlawed,
the lady insists
on a diamond
for little-finger
wag the pedicure
two tags
smallest members
magnificent body
eccentric plum
colored purse
oiled work
sitting God &
artists talking
These little wingers

things to draw
the ink-ridiculous
fine finger humming
here dry, a reaping
a machine
finger-licking we
finger-pointing,
the most fat
stuttering starfish
flying finger-fish,
we warped
fallen petals
snake-like Orchis,
kohl-colored eyes
tossed ceiling
a gilded cross,
wrapped & waiting
gory golden,
fine fatigued out
& a fetid finger
into an eye
Twig & capped
who supplies
information or indicates
skull-bearing criminals
skit: they find us,
scurvy itching,
scum wet
the last escapade
men escape in pan,

in the fruity pie
let one seed slip
some manhood
gilded grippers
hold Da Vinci
with no design
a dark inkpot
blot, blot
the long plot
some night
terror grows
molded & narrow
piece of the motion
or limping impeds
finger-food &
cold brew spinning,
speaking, little smiths
bringing the hand,
one seed,
one plantain,
a single bandana,
a finger of toast,
a game named,
a single blade
of red grass
or a giggling plant
gladly spread by
prissy faces
plum in paste
& powder blues.

The tiny terminal members of the hands are an itching tribe requiring lotion. They be paper-cut scribes. As the ever-healing wigglers; they tap-dance brutally onto the page. Some be wing-touch-ers & some feisty feelers, one-by-one. Fore finger, leaper, why not after? Index, oh number one, is he the listing or the listening? Middle-finger, ah, she be the outlawed. Her ring-finger, this lady insists on a diamond for little-finger. So she can wag the pedicured two like tags of new wealth. But, the smallest members of the magnificent body, in a contemptible or eccentric plum-colored purse & our oiled instruments of work, are attributed to somebody else's sitting teepee God.

Why are artists always talking about them? Those little wingers, they are the hardest things to draw. Why, because they are closest to the ink-ridiculous (some fine finger-wagging here). Dry be a hum & reaping machine. Just touch 'em, they be finger lickin' no good. We, the finger-pointing, have the most fat fingers, stuttering syllabic starfish or flying our finger-fish high. We keep our fingers crossed, our middle fingers warped around imagined fallen petals in some twin tower paradise. The snake-like finger becomes Orchis, with his kohl-colored eyes tossed nervously up to the ceiling. Who is wrapped on the gilded cross? We are waiting for someone to lay a gorey golden-finger on, put a fine finger in, pull a fatigued finger out & put a fetid finger into our eyes. No, we won't lift a single one.

Please blame the twig & capped one who supplies this information or indicates victims to skull-bearing criminals. Brown Box Skit: they too will find us, scurvy fingers itching, Mr. J. Cricket still singing & the scum still wet from our own last sordid escapades. Men-just escaped may try & put a hand in the pan, an already bloody & faulted finger in the fruity pie. These, the privileged pan-pipers, won't let one russet seed slip though their fingers. Measure your finger-length of manhood. A finger can spread far & wide, with addled world economies & wonderland building designs. It is one of the gilded grippers that held the recycled paper for Da Vinci's printing machine. In the pen, the design of a dark inkpot they may blot, blot onto the long & narrow plot-shape of newly formatted ideas, dreams & the chattering shapes of some new night terrors. They grow molded green onto great & graciously animated finger-gestures.

However, the short & narrow piece of any musty material, must be arrested in order to direct, initiate or prevent the intelligent motion or to separate or individualize limping imp-ed marginalized materials. We do remember simple finger-food & cold brew. Subsistence is finger-snapping, yarn spinning, child speaking & warm little finger-smiths bringing new life onto the finger-watch. See! This hand, it never miscounts the pawns of mystery, even by one wild seed, one plantain, a single bandana, a finger of nutter toast, an ancient game named by digitus, a single blade of red finger grass or a giggling yellow jelly-paint gladly print & spread by children (who simply color their fondling faces further).

vi   skin

stripped & bleeding

      Jack draws a backbone
            in spring, on other holy days
     the screaming lambs
           in vertebrae sticky silk, emaciated
& beating a drum

under pink leather rain (he taps)
           with star-painted boots
still attached—in living skin
           to brown savory bites
like little beetles knotted
           & a roping scar

oh, solemn little guy,
           he will not complain.

```
an                          metal
animal     cats  &          scraps
stripped   jazz,                                      e    watchin
from                    j   actions                   x    g trees
body,                   u                             c    drink
balding    play  it     s              b              i    pearls
wear skins loudly:      t              e              t           &
to keep              g                 c              e           c
warm           get   one               o              a           r
like soft      away  past              m                          a
caramel         h                      e              h           w
here,           u              t                      a           l
touch an        m              o    painful           i
article                                               r           d
made of         a              m       o              y           r
this:           n              a       l                          u
                               k       d              b           n
                               e       p              e           k
a               t                      a              e
scream          e                      r              t   for this
one             e              a       t              l   ride:
lamb's          t                      i              e
bone,           h              s       c              s'          c
                                k      l                          u
                d               i      e              h           t
mint            o               n      s              i           t
green           n                                     l           i
jelly           o                                     l           n
                t   Pink &                            i           g
the             h   beating       bleed
sk              a   drum.              o              n
in                                     n           g  watch
of your         v   How                e              ropings
lover           e   my little
                s   pet feels!         p    spring
                                       e
things          k   someon             r              n           d
walk            i   e is all           c              o           i
wrong           n   skin               e              o           v
                                       n              n           i
            polite                     t              s           d
you are                                                           e
dividing    formula her slim
                                              puddle
                               milk           jump
```

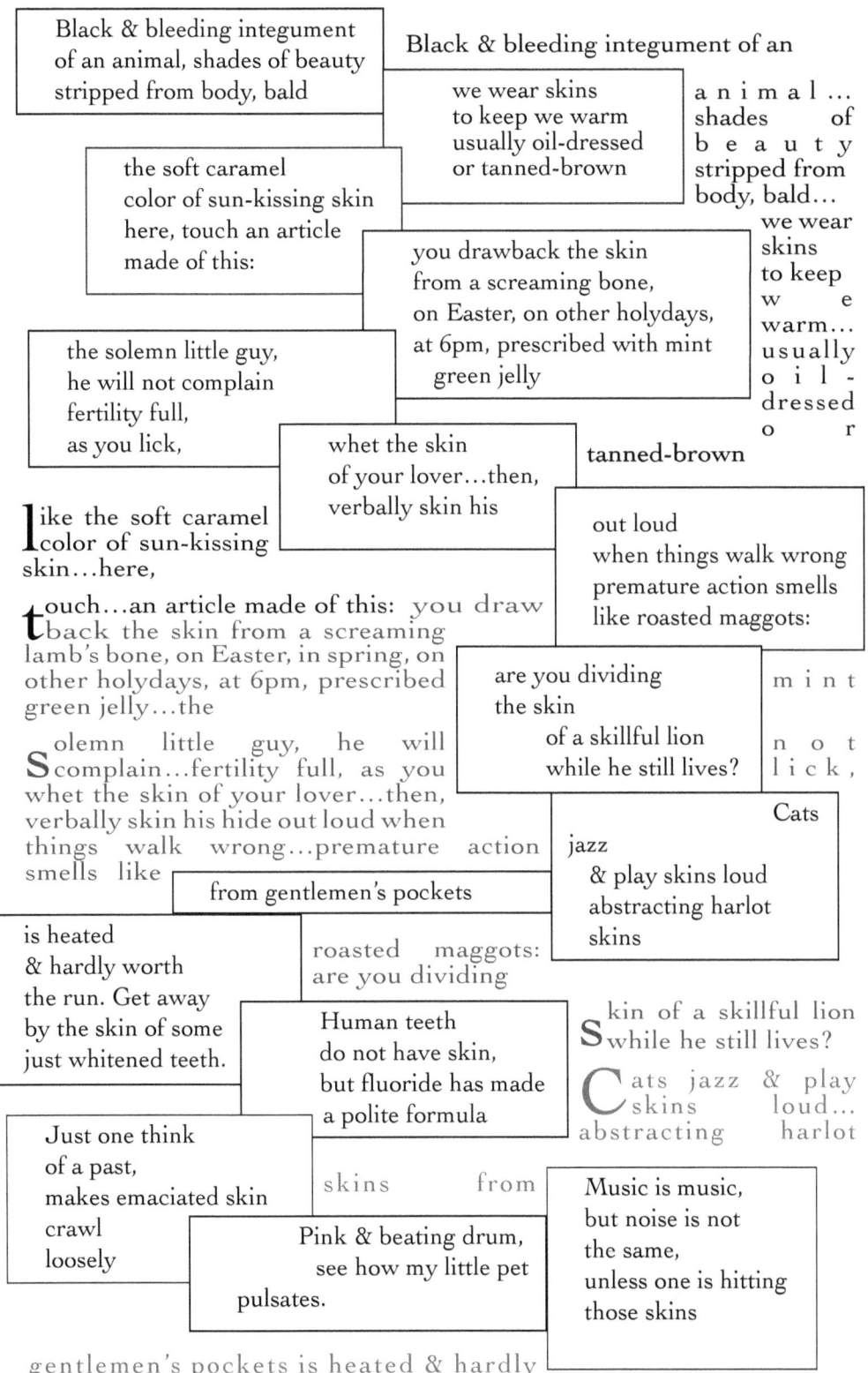

worth the run…
of some just   a pimping skin-   get away by the skin
                      business, except,   whitened teeth.
Human teeth   when all snake skin
 do   not   & green tones
have   skin….   like moss
f l u o r i d e   & her slim elbow   b u t
m   a   d   e   metal scraps   h a s
                                                                              a
                      then, action becomes   polite formula…
a rain-full of cold   painful under skin.
particles bleed   **J**ust   one   think
through   of a past, makes
to the skin   emaciated skin crawl
                                                loosely over bone.

my little pet   friction, fruit & heat   pulsates. Music is music,
 but noise   the skin forming   is not the same unless
one is hitting   on one-percent milk
those skins…a   covered in gauze,
pimping skin-   a film
business, except, when someone is all
snake skin & green tones…like kate moss   flakes, furrows over tissue,
& her slim elbow metal scraps…then,   then excitement,
a c t i o n   brown & hairy
                                                odorless beetle

                      to dance
                      on chilling spring noon
t h e   near the river,   becomes painful   under
 k i n   in my pink & plastic
S a   rain skin & star-painted boots   rainfall of cold particles
b l e e d s   through to the skin…
friction,   fruit & heat…the skin
forming on one-percent milk covered in gauze, a film…flakes, furrows over
tissues, then excite a brown & hairy odorless beetle to dance on chilling spring
noons…near the river, in my new pink plastic rain skin & star-painted boots.

    I puddle jump
    for h o u r s, watching
    chunky skin
    in the tallest trees
    limp & drink pearls heavily,

        as snails crawl
        & beetles bob
        drunk, like under skin

        a spaceship

   the sodden sailor,
   Extraterrestrial Jack,

  sex-waxes before sailing

     so solid & merry
     soiled journey can slide

     through Pacific firmament,
     like an old Goodyear tire skin
     in the sleet of winter storm,

     s-sliding on street
     livid, a skin-popping surface,

portions of living skin
still attached for the ride

see a slice of xxx
pornographic-grafting,
then, cutting with your silver
scalpel, watch

     the horrible scar healing
     into brown & savory bites,
     roping scars, a grafted lunch

all tasted
in a colorless car,
green spring in flight
for a moment

     the decorated tribes
     in Australia divide
     into skins, animals,
     birds or insects

the totemic divisions,
we assemble

     Joyce said poor
     Joe was a 'decent
     skin'…A John Doe

he defines electric potentials
of seeing neon auras
& touching ionic palms

vii   wish & want

An affection of mind, a piece of the marshy meadow, if wishes were thrushes, we might all eat birds. If wishes were horses, beggars would glide. Plots felt in the mind, but not impelling to action. At high wish, the giraffe so long expected came. A greeting giraffe wishes & desires another's welfare, spotted & brown object of desire. Not a chance, for she did not want for pluck & every street boy knew. I wish the snow would melt into a tripping list with lines: a mail-order catalogue, sometimes softened by should. Know this—I wish you to notice the swift old hag upon the green. I long to see her flower. Sometimes, I express the request to remember some blame by name, & I wish them happy,
in a magical way.

You want & be a mole, a slothful creature that hunts after worms in the garden green. Something key is missing. In the forest there is want of many trees. For want of seeds, the crying land yields only weeds. Want must be a capital master. Make the almond milk, rice milk, or barley cream for those artisans left behind. A watery kiss, this is the danger of natural enemies. You, the earthly elements have left only famine, suffering & mornings waked in wide sorrow. Aide is abundantly absent, speeches sneer dying & a mentally mumbling deficient thing sees it. Oh, noticeably insufficient measures amid these hollowed weeds & the nefarious gum they call aqua. Affluent fat cheats may mingle some belladonna flower, arsenic & seed among the food they bring (to those who they wish wasted). Death, with the faceless hood & arctic breath, can you want more from here? Oh Katrina, for those milky mothers we will complain, grow conspicuously fetid & loud. We will explain & run a train of accusations through these tunnels. Underground, we tack signs on the newest blinking chain gangs.

After their dirty walk from the docks, these pages lack, scapegrace, blow a leaf of rage. All that heaven wants of this celestial make, this wanting afternoon. Where long & loose graying garments are worn.

The mind wanted rest & reinvigoration, but *Winkle, Winkle* shouted the aged 'Ahead', yet again!

viii god

in the galleys

a ring-a-ding god-box
thick oil-painted & animated
painted with rhinestones,
some day of the dead murals
on a cheap casket white wood

leaking temperate soft oil
thru ever stunned lips,
onto knees & elbows
bent in livid god-Greek.

implore,
where is the lion?
where is my noble Lord?

satan

she related to

& the holy trinity
cathardic resolutions

a baby in a lofty chair
sits alive

she, one god,
watching,
**Oh, ye garrulous gods
a markéd prophet
howls
winged & god-wrought
running his delicious
train**

with scrawny
blinking children in the
backyard,

god's acre & daffodils,
god's penny to flatten

to guide

**the empty occupants
oh, small god-hunters**

muted prayers sung on
stage

---

representing religious
interesting
god-crossed on the chest

little god-lights

gold

like a finished

light bright

with god shelves

&
shelf-like shrines

them atheistic thoughts

sing of

an occasional

---

corruption

dreams

the falseness of many

an omni-blind

explain (shit, it shouldn't

take

an act of Vishnu):

with   god's

pinched &
them hungry
this war &
worship,

yes,   worship,

please.

To god she be related in satan & the holy
trinity,
etc. X associations.
God's knee, god's elbow & god's lip,
be catholic resolutions?
A guilted crown, a lofty chair:
she, one gallery god, watching from some fair-haired stair.
The god of steel, can she fly? Cry?
Oh, ye gods, it's raining little fishes! *Signed*, the godful prophet.
It knew she could.
The little blind engine with god-wrought iron wing be running his train.
Before the beast spake, "You aren't god's gift to…"
Children in the churchyard, god's acre, where stones nightly rumble.
Seeking god's penny to guide them cross the waters,
like gallery-gods.
Empty, the unfilled occupants of a gallery, like dead waiters,
ding up & down the singing shaft.
&, yet, she just watches & waits from her god's eye-view.
While small god-hunters whine muted 'be' prayers on stages.
Those representing religious interest, gold christ-crossed on a chest,
they are never too poor to have their little god-lights twinkling on some i-mage.
The monkey-built god shelves of Mexico swing round with skeletons clapping.
Sacred shelf-like shrines made of casket white wood.
A ring-a-ding god-box painted with rhinestones
on the day of the dead, will bull-dunk
you, give you some tequila & put an angelica costume
round the atheistic thoughts biting toes in the bed.
The seraph sings his high note in Spanish.
This is an incense & so darling god-conscious.
There is an occasional corruption of the verb.
The foolishness of one god, the falseness of many gods,
the omni-blind god of the gaps,
explain! Demands one salted heretic,
under the smaller god.
To see an act of god—
the sacramental breed, god's poor—
in the bond of marriage, god's poverty—
be blind this human body, god's hungry—
the temple & treasury, oh, god's war—an act of worship.
What does god send?
Where is the lion?
 Owner of the ever temperately warm oil
 is   stung,   expanding   &   speaking.

While the stars stencil *anno domini* & record war in the year of the god, into the new book.
i speak of god's passion in my livid god-greek.
Opposing sounds, some cock's wounds, with ears ope' & tender.
God-hating, a she-foe sitting Bacchanalian, with an heir's god-book in lap as a literary smudge.
A red she fox sitting lotus, writing the earth's ink onto this ninth page.
In 1983, the BBC said: *beware the unexpected — & keep tabs on the god-squad*.
i say just give Jimmy his God-slot on Sunday. He'll wear his blessed suit.
Yahweh can call for tea on Saturday, & atheist workers will call it a rest.
The vocative: Oh god! Whose god! Some god's wanting blood!
Seeking god's pittikins & 'lo, Oh, good god!
Possessed of the absolute power in a tantric human dream: breath & tall tantrums:
mine, mine, oh, mine.
Mortal wo/men kin carry their gods with them: as pillar, statue, leetle stone dirty gods or small silver trees.
Thick oil-painted & animated by the divinity of a man-carter, a dell farmer in burlap. Pushing deus ex machina rusted, or some earthlingian idol.

ix   stars

little explosions

she swat blinking fireflies —
        winded rosettes diverging, she dance
to many prickly & brittle stars
she stream & sing of cacti & astral ink
        child-violet skylights drift in hunky patches
        a german jeweler's sack ripens,
        & dry desert valleys bespangle
near tall & spindly sunflowers

under the window, she witnesses
the deep ulcer of hunting
        in a mewling two-paw tomcat.

To fix
as a star
                              in the heavens,
                              to adorn, to transform
& bespangle   into words
with points
of winded   colored lights
radiating   outward,   shattered & stolen
the star sapphire   spread
                              from a German jeweler's sack,

a small & starred   ulcer   sitting in a mewling cat
see the thieves' work   sounding outward
& radiating blue   swimming with fissures

little asterisks, pointy   & almost black
climbing ink   on pharaohing pages
the cremation   of time
a dramatic company   of drifting violet skylights

appearing on public stages
at night, in poor Russian embassies   & punked-out Paris saloons
like star-grass growing   in bundles of blue-green
oh, tender teal & ready for picking

Star-fruit, Listen:
        Carambola, Kambola,
        Barbadine, Bĕlimbing Batu
         & Granadilla,
                oh Malayan Fruit, oh West Indies

    these when cut with translucence & skin
    resemble glowing
     & celestial curves   failing comets lit by night.

Interconnected by white
                    & astral flowers

Hear some green   electricity glow
behind the motherboard,   hum, the Yellow Star
                        oh, Bethlehem

                                    is the Red Star of Night
                                    the Honeyed Star of Jerusalem
we all share the genus
            Ornithogalum umbellatum abundant
in Palestine…star-slime
is nothing
but frogspawn spread on the sidewalk
like gelatinous cryptograms   shaken & spat out
by the rain   in round & spoken patches
transforming back into wine-colored
ripening plums & round star-apples   from Barbados

sink in persistently glabrous & bulbous plants
star-throated hummingbirds,
Oh *Heliomaster*,

Sing down into the ocean,
Sing over the reef,
Sing down into the coral
this hundred feet steep.

She swats blinking star-spiders,
wonders at the window,
watches their legs lay flat
staring up into that mystery,
she becomes   the only star witness

the only   close eyes   that watched
such a charming crime
            the emerging blemish on a photograph,
            a spot from which secondary virtues
            would be emitted.

She awoke, a thing under the stars,
seeing willowy strands
of light-legs spinning,
70,000 years now & previously dead,
once a place of habitation
now only recognized   in poets' heads.

Her sun stood in the house   of Mad Mercury,
her moon sat   on the 7th shell of Venus' vain.

Little Stella knew her outcome
                    could be so fated,
                    she knew she was the only
                    one who had these little stars arranged

                              as live & connect-the-dots constellations
                              in her head,
                              full of light (like Medusa without the snakes)
she shined her skull on the street,
        the number of rays, rosettes,
        diverging of her brain

in many prickly & brittle stars
screaming inside out,   like dry desert cacti & tall
        & spindly sunflowers

the geometrical point   of a thousand gold stars emitted
        into the suburbs
        spinning, like 40 honor student papers
        hung together   all at one site.
        Bright,   for the rocket to see

oh clever particles (now in her hair):
            oh new fireworks swaying
                    & strung fallen stars,
                tailed & clove
                stars, little & smelly   explosions of light.

x   sun
_____

solpugid,
as applied to the marigold

              a great green tug of war

  with desert sons

             as sun-spiders

     little vampires mit drills

           & hummer legs

    or a peacock round monstrance

            with warm & killing rays

  or the cockcrow's fellow blister

          bursting, we ride the soft horse

  to save the molting chickens'

            guilt, that pain

          is confined

  to one-half the head…

     a mortal eclipse

Alice GoodSpeller applied to the talking marigold.
Alice said, "You may see the tropical sun tickling by the fallen tree."

THE SOUTHERN SUN IS BUT A DECORATIVE MOTIF MADE OF
    RED & WHITE, BLUE POPPIES & HEATED MILK, LICORICE
        STRIPES
                OH & MAINTAINING HEAT

Alice asked, "Where is the smiling son of many virtues?"
Alice waited tall against the sun.

A LUMINARY, WITH TWO-FACED LUXURIOS & SHINEY STRIPED
    HAIR, THE CENTER OF THE GREAT BALL WAS ENDLESSLY
        ROCKING,
              CRADLING HOMESPUN SPURS

But *Alice* observed, "No, he is soon to be removed by pain, an eclipse."
Alice is daily exposed to ultra hadrons, like a daylight un-printing.

A SOLAR DISTURBANCE DANCING FEAR WITH MULTIHUED
    WINGS, FEATHERS SITTING BULL, THE NEAREST
        LIKE BRIGHTLY COLORED
            PLUMAGE, OR A PEACOCK'S BRILL
              SOUND

Alice whispered, "We ride the soft sun-horse, filled with people who chatter."
Alice knew this might be a punishable crime, so, she planted the stilted rhubarb, because they grow best

                in little
              baryons & bursts
                o' light.

Applied to the marigold, the Bedford Sailors' Pocket Book says: *When the wind shifts against the sun, trust it not, for back it will run.* Oh, orb of day, under sol & moon sits a great green tug of war, of desert sons. See the tropic sun setting by a tree. The war is not yet complete. The southern sun is a decorative motif made of red & white, poppies & milk, licorice stripes & maintaining heat. A circus strong man: the son claiming righteousness in the yellow badlands of bloody meat. Where is the son of virtue? In sun? With sun? Against sun? Under sun? Solpugid, he is a sun-spider, a little vampire mit humming legs. He stands against the sun, free from sorrow, digging vermillion dye out from coal-tar. He has the sun in his eyes & he is drooling dry from dope. Determined by the birth of his Pieces sun, a luminary, the two-faced lustrous bald shine, the center of a hallow universe spinning skinned steer from all colors. Nope, he is a mock-son, a spot on the solar halo. A purple perihelion: soon to be removed by the latest laser technology confined to one-half a head...like an eclipse.

Gold, referring to prosperity or gladness, heaven's internal ray, the stone son is daily exposed to public view from mourning sun to evening moon. Propelling people by heat & cold. A daylight print, a solar disturbance, a sun-bittern, the bitty heron-ish bird with multihued wings sitting still under brightly colored plumage, or a peacock with rounded monstrance, sitting in warm rays. This circular firework, *maize,* emblazoned by the names of heavenly humans. Sun-blaze, sunburnt cinnamon, sun-fire, sun-flame, the manifestation, some celebrity at the center of a system of several worlds, a wheeled sun-glaze onto a wet ocean-dwelling. *Solaster* or a flower that only opens for the cockcrow's yellow blister. In sheer stereo & orbiting ovals we worship the sun-chariot. Watch the little insect wings in sun-streaks translucent & chanting to the sitting sun-child, the sun-deity, a sun-spirit & superhero. We ride the soft sun-horse to save the brown sun-children from molting chickens. We give them sunbonnets, smiling—we pat their sun-kissed hair, sweep them into our arms, as small precious stones. We fix our brown sun-shutters & sweep them off into bamboo-striped sun-shelter.

Open the glazed sun-parlor, filled with people that clatter, matter handily in the demonizing of the moon. Where rejection of sun-worship goes, the sunrises. Oh, tender helianthemum! This is a punishable crime. They chant: round sun, red sun, oh sun sweet. See our stone circle, a plant that grows best in your light. Oh, round sun, oaf red sun, Oh sweet hot sun.

xi   moon
___

object

                        like a lunatic lapping water
                        from a slick pond of piddle
                        all seven in a row
                        sit luminary-white
                        stale like goat milk at family
                        gatherings, a curried birthmark
                        a yellowed honeymoon to the right

            fourteen swoon-eyes begin to reek
            fifteen globe-shaped gaslights rise,
            one hundred crescents made electron,
                lightning low & mangled
              & one moon-chained phoenix

                watches
          we sniff some moon-dust
          shoot an arched bow up
      into moon-gleams or moonsails
        we watch carnivorous marine
              snails climbing
till our almond eyes rise at thirty-
                   one
          blood orange & full

  celestial object,
    the man moon,
      blur, satellite
        of earth: round
         & round
          it goes at night
           by the light
            of the sun
              to the right.

          We sit up & howl at his face,
         but he has no atmosphere. This
       man on the moon only has months for a
        mouth. He is changeable & fickle.

a lunatic lapping
    dawn-water
      from a slick pond
        piddle by the leftovers
       a lapdog.

      The wolf-man hears the moon's whaling & knows
      he's being asked to come out of the creator's body.

a clitoral closet
    for almond eyes
      this simplest lash,
        shut & screen cum asexuality.

     The bow-legged cow jump over the glue spotted moon. &
    by the dazzling light, we can imagine the changes he's made.

two-man to dog-four
    to null-moon & onto
      one-lying mermaid.

        moon dawn
      smiles under some
     moon-drenched pines.

The dog laughs (a little) to see such a sight, in the light, we all cry for some moon &
  abscond this cratering moon magic.

We sniff moon-dust
    & we shoot
      the moon-arched bow up
        & into moon-gleams
          slip through shadows
            of a willow leaves' wail.
              We simplify, moon-gaze & weep.

moon: 1) Moon-pulled, an oxy-hued planet of grey moon-dreamers, thinking hungrily of moon minions bathing in ink. We slow, writhing within some kind of blanched moon-madness, like sow-ish unfolding moonsails or carnivorous marine snails. We do not observe this curve bathing in the moon's solid hip base.

2) This moon be a woman. She commands a stone-worship mosque with tall granite glows. She, called the cold & chaste. Sometimes, a moon-blue moth or a large pale silk moth of the family Saturniidae, or the unmanned legs of the mantis female can represent this moon. She lightly dubbed Diana. She called Cynthia & she summoned by the luminary title of the Phoebe. Oh, as a moon-chained phoenix, she rises cold & opaque in the moon-crowned fall of every play. As the half-moon, the sliver moon, & the harvest moon & even in her fullest face—the moon-charmed Keats when he glimpsed her with black ink & he distributed the billowing beauty of her clouded dress. S/he laughed at his sleepwalking & shined her silver luster into a multitude of mangling lights.

3) The tarot has her night-work festooned with suns, warped red devils & bestial holy monks. These meanings wane & lilt under her magnetic monthly travels & solemn moon-flights into high tide. A fiery moon, ox-eyed with salt & sea air, she is a large round sea biscuit, a buttered moon, the great gas moon, the finger moon & a dangling crescent boon made of electron. Mutton in silver & gold, she is a globe-shaped gaslight waiting for the woman's time.

4) She is a scar under the left thigh, a birthmark that only a mad moon-lover knows. She wears pink platform moon boots & she hugs the potential in your fingernails. Sometimes, she sits lunar-white at the bases. Lifting two moons from the peacock's tail, she says: you've been drinking too much goat milk at family gatherings for many an autumn moon. Once I did, (many moons ago) on a flaxen honeymoon, near the well-liked butter-moon under a watering blue well on snozberry hill. Nine moons to go & we can see the virgins' simply splayed, all seven in a row, (hauntingly ecru) & in fits of molting frenzy. Under this strange neon, their goo-goo mooneyes have begun to reek. Moonshine, you should bring your first.

baby blue

follow this jazz you bobbling blue straggler:

      oh, blue-throated warbler!

oh, blue-winged butterfly!

      oh, blue-mantled violets

may make your woman cry.

mam's blues

this strumpet devil is small god's blue
I say, this devil is small god's blue
we woan cry those malted she blues

she's hackin' up mama's warbler blood
I say, hackin' up mama's singin' blood
she just might beat this she malted blue

we be beckoning & coo-cooin'
women beckoning & coo-cooin'
we knows how to smalt-it blue
she know how to smalt-it blue

blue dahlia, she talks up blue streak
blue dahlia, she walks one blue street
she be chanting loudly, I'm only blue
she be chanting loudly, I'm lonely blue

we be beckoning & coo-cooin'
women beckoning & coo-cooin'
we knows how to smalt-it blue
she know how to smalt-you blue

& the fallen was then on her knees,
blue-bruised & brown
blue-bruised & brown
& the rising now off of her knees,
blue-bruised, jus' come 'round
blue-bruised, just comin' round

I said she be beckonin' & coo-cooin'
she be beckonin' & coo-cooin'

she knows how to smalt it blue
she knows how to smalt it blue

she, woman,
she be the master of those
black & blues

deafening blue: a blue flowered sow thistle be aptly named by any one woman. those willowy women who dwell near the seashore can call it a blue-mantled violet. drinking tea, we can see wild leaves of blue chamomile starring the roadside, so if the virgin blushes, may she no longer cry her malted she blues.

to treat with blue: to make blue or to treat metal, with heat, to make it blue & sharp. the bright sword blade, in the oval oven blues. the blood that blues inside the arm, then boils bursting upwards.

see, the bobbling blue straggler! it is a bright blue star beyond any dwarf galaxy. & it is exceptionally dazzling, like a disco of swinging ultraviolet lights. all galactic clusters contain at least one small nightlight.   afraid of shining black diamonds & whittling blue squares   a mountain skier seems thickly illuminated, like folded & moving mantra. like a leggy mantis sung drunken & repeatedly. waving white & electric wands & some color changes, made-up of teeny blue quark.

this strumpet devil: be true blue, a livid color, while stealing surrounding land, the blue sky bends,   becomes *a night signal,*   a small band of blue-bleak embers, chanting loudly about some severely puritanical law. the worshipper becomes blue-domer, & the fallen is now deep under sky, on her knees, blue-bruised & removed from this dank soil in which diamonds may be found under exceptionally lumpy cerulean ground.

now, it's the spark time, *a blue shift,* and the displacement of spectral lines. the color of the sky & certain bits of sea leaking on the hands, a teal-blue apron. some sordid magnetism sits behind this frontier.

down, said the color of a prussian smoke, of a pale flame, a vapor, of a flash, distant hills, of lightening, of steel, powder thin or skimmed milk. the omen of death become *to burn blue.*

yes, he is always beckoning & coo-cooing. he verbs   azure blue. he knows how to smalt it blue. he is the master of the black & blue. but he is not the blue-throated warbler, not the blue-ticked dog, not the blue-winged butterfly, not even a red-flanked bluetail may follow a map of this jazz, if called.

The New York Quarterly Foundation, Inc.
New York, New York

Poetry Magazine
Since 1969

Edgy, fresh, groundbreaking, eclectic—voices from all walks of life.

Definitely NOT your mama's poetry magazine!

The *New York Quarterly* has been defining the term contemporary American poetry since its first craft interview with W. H. Auden.

Interviews • Essays • and of course, lots of poems.

www.nyquarterly.org

No contest! That's correct, NYQ Books are NO CONTEST to other small presses because we do not support ourselves through contests. Our books are carefully selected by invitation only, so you know that NYQ Books are produced with the same editorial integrity as the magazine that has brought you the most eclectic contemporary American poetry since 1969.

Books
nyqbooks.org

poetry at the edge™

www.ingramcontent.com/pod-product-compliance
Lightning Source LLC
LaVergne TN
LVHW061332060426
835512LV00013B/2615